POETIC PARADISE

BRITTA EVELYN

ISBN: 979-8-9923416-0-7 (Ebook)

ISBN: 979-8-9923416-1-4 (Hardback)

ISBN: 979-8-9923416-2-1 (Paperback)

THEMES

I. THE ARTS

Take My Picture
Art
Muses Prayer
Poetry
Our Music Continues
Dance
Act it Out
The Inspired One
Healing Sounds

II. NATURE

Pool of Tears
Solar Power
Rose
Outshine Darkness
Shadow
Transmute
The Young Moon
It's all Inside
Butterfly
Loyal Companion

III. LIFE, LOVE AND LOSS

Hearts Reflection
Friend
You Are My Everything
True
Gentleman in Green
Gone but Forgotten
Main Character
The Woman Who Named Me
Lily Dreams
Butterfly Child
Unchained
That Shine

IV. PEACE, WISDOM, AND TIME

Ties
Medal of Dishonor
Time
Key
Nova
Ripple
Searching
25
Peace
Generation Harmony
Wisdom
Secret Angel
My Dearest Readers

I

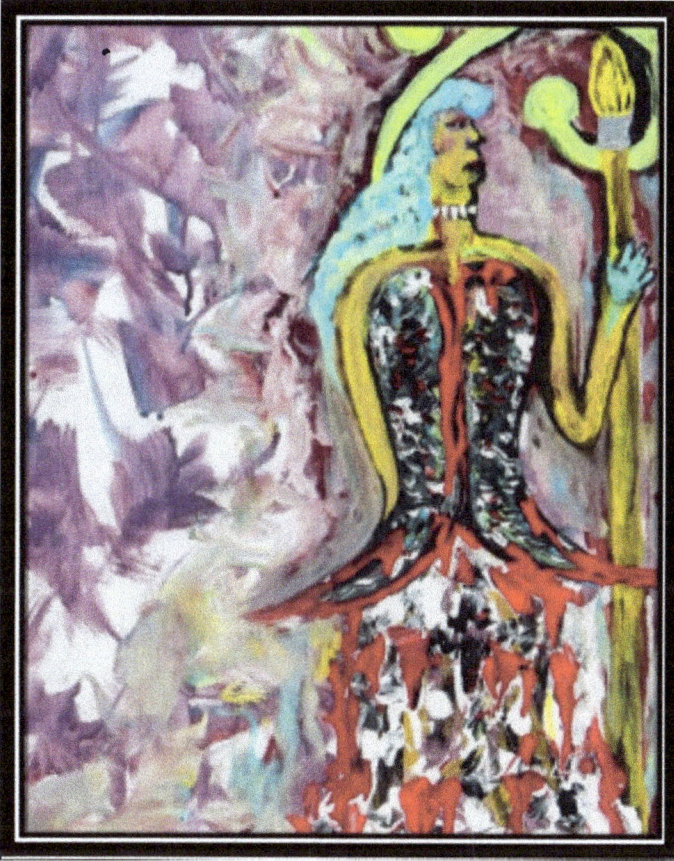

THE ARTS

TAKE MY PICTURE

A photo marks a place in time

Capturing a memory in its prime

Remember a party or even a birth

Look back at the time loved ones were still on this Earth

After the photo is taken, we resume what we are doing

When acting for the camera

Is it fame we are pursuing?

So, you may take my picture and make it a good shot

A picture makes a memory even more than just a
thought

ART

Art is a life force

True creators don't destroy

They bring worlds together

Transform sadness into joy

MUSES PRAYER

I am the stage on which the Muses perform

They create wonder above me from evening to 'morn

As the vessel below I hear all that they say

Their magical words incite me to pray,

"Muses above me please teach me your song, your creativity is endless, and your talents are strong. My senses are an open blossom, your inspiration helps me grow, and together we will give the world the most divine show."

POETRY

You could write out your feelings
Ride out your fears
You could do this for a living
Make a good dollar this year
What is the purpose?
If any might be found
To pen these broken thoughts
Giving mute papers a sound
The purpose is finding meaning
When all else is lost
Save the sinking ship
When the Captain jumped off
Someone had to pave the way
Bringing first fire to our literary cave
So put everything into it
Seize this creative day!
Pen down words and letters
Let me show you the way
Find beauty, even sorrow
Take note and express outwardly

The end result is a picture

Painted by your heart, powerfully

OUR MUSIC CONTINUES

It started long ago in a field of grass

When our music went quiet

You revived the past

We were a family

Uniting our neighbors in song

An Opry was built

Though the road was quite long

Our music was the melody of the woods

Carried upon trees as they swayed

You'll see us in your memory

With each song you replay

Celebrating our music

And the talent we've showed

It's the greatest honor for the hard work we've sowed

If heaven exists, we're smiling from above

You shared our passion with many

Thanks to your labor of love

__DANCE__

I am called to dance

Like a bee inside its hive

Carrying a message

My feet, they come alive

Bending and raising

Leaping up and down

Call me the Queen of Dance

I'll gladly wear that crown

ACT IT OUT

Show up early and get your makeup done

Remember your lines

We stay until this scene is done

Call cut

Do it again

Show more emotion this time

Good thing you have the method

You aren't just a mime

Acting is an honor

To tell another's story

Let someone else write it

You deserve your fame and glory

THE INSPIRED ONE

Given secret knowledge as a child

With colorful dreams his mind ran wild

He was chosen to set the people free

From misery and locked-mind disease

His sacred writings and music touched the seeking

On wild medicine he met sages while his journey was peaking

The Dreamer knew his gift could only be carried so far

Since masses sought out to make him a star

The jealous put him on their radar

They wanted to sever the angel's wings

Arrow the crow so it no longer sings

The Dreamer made a choice to silence his body's voice

In flowing water nearby

The Dreamer said goodbye

Earth people wondered why, and all began to cry

Dreamer said from now I'll bring wisdom from the sky

Seeking hearts may know my word

I'll send it down through the songs of the bird

HEALING SOUNDS

Music is a healing gift
It sends pain far away
Every beat is a treated bandage
Medication, the melody you play
Never allow the world to grow quiet
Musicians don't you stop
We need you more than ever now
Become like a stone, and rock!

II

<u>NATURE</u>

THE POOL OF TEARS

There once was a pool of tears

Over the years it collected human worries and tears

The plants cried, "Pool don't be greedy, us trees and
flowers are needy!"

Let us grow strong

In our roots tears belong

Finally, the pool poured out

Its contents soaked the land

The tears traveled to all the plants

Towards their roots, up every strand

The tears made them grow taller

Their branches widened fifty feet longer

So next time you weep

Let the tears drop past your feet

Mother Nature takes your burdens

And in the depth, she keeps

When up grand roots these tears do seep

You'll gain release and healing

From the beauty of nature

Her gifts are ever so often revealing

SOLAR POWER

Blonde star above me today

You are lovely in every way

Smiling always

You're a brilliant ray

Shining brightly upon our world

Every single day

Never let your light go out

You keep this world a' going

Life benefits from you making such a brilliant showing

<u>ROSE</u>

Can't you see her standing there?

An elegant flower, so beautifully rare

She attracts bees as she sways under trees

Stands strongly in place as sunshine kisses her face

Within this season she will come and go

Sure, she grew high but did she ever-

She rose!

OUTSHINE DARKNESS

For a time, they were one

The Moon and the Sun

They spent each day in bliss

No other closeness such as this

Like a flash they were torn apart

A new life alone was to start

Moon didn't understand why

Ripped apart without goodbye

What Moon didn't know is how they were both needed

Growth and new purpose this separation seeded

Sun saw this change as a new horizon

Its sacrifice, a new future lies in

They were given their new role

To shine bright from their soul

Earth needs warmth to exist and grow

Only their light is strong enough to show

Since they're both unique and have great love

It's their purpose to grace Earth from above

Moon and Sun begin their new task

Hiding their emotions behind glowed mask

The Sun sinks down to sleep at night

Leaving the Moon to shine its white light

Each time the Sun drops below the equator

Moon is impacted with another crater

Moment has come for sleepy Moon to go to bed

Sun shines bright in moon's memory overhead

Being apart makes them morn

Missing their loved one causes forlorn

But they must keep on going

For Earth, they keep on showing

The bigger picture is displayed clearly

Although it's hard, Earth needs them dearly

Each shining so bright

One in day

One in night

If Sun gave up from mourning

It would take away Earth's morning

If Moon lost its bravery like knight

Earth would be in darkest night

Sometimes the longing makes them want to end

Their hearts keep going because they are a light for a
friend

Seeing past sadness makes hope appear

Loved ones might be far, but their love is still here

SHADOW

Shadow is created from light

Gains its camouflage during night

Shadow doesn't wait in the distance

It's at your feet in every instance

Shadow is a part of you

From your head down to shoe

If you miss your Shadow, remember it's there

Not just behind you, but everywhere

As long as you've existed, Shadow's been your guide

Whenever the light hits your face

Guess who's by your side?

TRANSMUTE

When you are weeping

I am the tree you should be seeking

Give me a hug and start speaking

Into my trunk let your worries begin releasing

Deep into my roots let your tears be seeping

Your anguish and burdens I will be keeping

Transmuting them into healing emotions

Of which you will be reaping

THE YOUNG MOON

Good morning, Moon

Haven't seen the light of day

Little Moon

I hope you're here to stay

Bright Sun comes over

And takes your glory away

So sad is my Little Moon

Little Moon,

See what you must do?

Find someone who lets you be you

See me here looking up at you?

Don't you know Little Moon,

That you shine too?

When night is here

And Sun passes away

It's your time Little brightly Moon

To come out and play!

So, love Little Moon

And shine with all your might!

You know who will come to see you

Every single night

IT'S ALL INSIDE

Everything has a subtle beat

Feel it pulsing under your feet

Mother Nature does call

To the souls that will not fall

Help her in her dismay

Guide others to see greater change

It's all inside

Though you may not see

The little ways it's meant to be

Please, see in your heart

It's all inside

To be the one who always tries

Be the stars in a world of black

And never once, ever, look back

BUTTERFLY

Her feet are dark from the Earth

A free spirit from birth

Butterfly dance

Entranced

She sings

Open wings

Flying high

Amongst forever sky

Transformation complete

Fluttering with nature's beat

LOYAL COMPANION

Little footsteps trailing behind

Never a creature so purely divine

Your eyes tell me what you hold in your heart

My kindred spirit from the very start

Though your life is much too short

Your days are never in vain

Your happiness is my therapy

A shelter from the rain

Wherever I go, there you will be

An ever-loyal buddy

My friend for all eternity

Now how'd you get all muddy?

III

LIFE, LOVE AND LOSS

HEART'S REFLECTION

Lying there at the base of my chair

Admiring your long chestnut hair

You're full of wonder

My love grows fonder

At my feet like roots

Touching my boots

How I love to shine down my rays of intention

For you, my heart's reflection

FRIEND

A confident rebirth
Lone flower once wilted
Now strong in this Earth
I wonder if our paths hadn't crossed
How deeply I'd be lost?
I often think about the rain
The way it kills a drought
Your caring is a refreshing shower
Its impact, don't you doubt
No words on Earth do exist
For what my heart wants to speak
To express what you mean to me
Only actions I can seek
So, when your sky is blue or grey
Call me anytime or day
I'll land on your shoulder
As a Monarch in spring to brighten your way
God made a friendship
Stronger than steel
Making us better
A bond that is real
As we go on this journey

I hope that we'll find
Everything that we seek
In the constructs of time
Family, friends, and love
Make a person feel blessed
Having you as my friend
Means that I have the best

<u>YOU ARE EVERYTHING</u>

You are the world before

And the world to come

You are the anthem

And the song to be sung

You are loved

Far beyond the sands

That cover Egypt

And past exotic lands

Show everyone

Who you envision to be

No time like the present

Attendance is mandatory

<u>TRUE</u>

You didn't look down on me
When I was giving up
Giving love in plenty
Filling my cup
Friends like you
Are so hard to find
Devotion so true
Your spirit so kind
Others won the title
But don't want the bother
Put on a show, a recital
They feed decaying fodder
Thank you for being here
To keep me intact
I will always be near
Our bond stronger than pact
My dear friend forever
Every day shall you smile
Any storm we will weather
In our own perfect style

GENTLEMAN IN GREEN

Run away, run away
Fair gentleman in green
Run away, run away
Not so callous as you seem
Today might be the day
You face your fears and smile
Won't you indulge your heart
And grace us for a while
Fear makes you slither
And push others away
Perhaps you won't dance tomorrow
But won't you dance today?
Love from afar, love from afar
Love from far away
Won't you come closer Dear?
Allow yourself to stay
This unspoken thing between us
It sure divides the way
Coming across as such a fuss
Resolve comes at delay
Today is right, today is wrong
That all depends on you

No such gentleman is so unique

So mysterious as you

Ever pervading in my every thought

As I often say you can

Never in all of history

Was there ever such a man

The story ends on a simple note

This gentleman in green

His stature stood before me

Down is the bridge he built between

So long fear

And so long sorrow

Life grows here and it's evergreen

We dance today

And we dance tomorrow

Me and my gentleman in green

GONE BUT FORGOTTEN

Your name is unfamiliar to me
Your eyes I no longer see
You are just a faded memory
Together we used to be
But we are no longer in each other's company
Love between us could not be
Our match was not matched perfectly
The problem is that you are you
And I am me
We each live our lives so differently
I chose freedom
You chose prison
You have fallen
While I have risen
If only you had opened your heart
You and I wouldn't have made our part
If only you had opened your eyes
But now you are the one who cries
If only you had opened your mind

You wouldn't be in this bind

Opposites may attract

But it's love that keeps it intact

MAIN CHARACTER

Do you lie amongst the Lilac fields
Smelling the scent of your own cologne?
Do you look down your nose while perched on your gold throne?
Who do you think you are?
A diamond in the rough?
A gem like you wouldn't even make the cut
The Earth does not bend to meet the feet of just your shoes
You'd think you were a circle in a basket full of cubes
You love only yourself
Oh, what a relationship that must be!
But it's kind of crowded, no?
There's you, yourself, and me, me, me!

THE WOMAN WHO NAMED ME

Springtime came new life
Cold seasons to an end
Many were presented
A new name to amend
This name was once adorned
By a sweet child long ago
Her life cut short quickly
Old age she never sewed
To keep her memory alive
Her name looked for a home
Sweet and kind as the home before
Many children never drew near it
But a heart it finally saw
March the eighth
Or somewhere near it
The time it finally called
How blessed this child is
Her name landing as a feather
Softly down upon the baby's chest
Forever to be tethered
To the woman that named me

I hope I make you proud

And bring smiles to the faces that speak our name out loud

LILY DREAMS

Lily dreams
Petals of white
You laid a Lily
Atop my body tonight
Over crossed arms
It softly laid
Eyes watering down upon it
When final respects were paid
This Lily will wither
Like my delicate fibers will
Don't blink or you'll miss it
The view of my spirit
Soaring beyond the windowsill

BUTTERFLY CHILD

There are spirits in her hair
Butterfly wings she likes to wear
A unique and multicolored pair
Winds whisper in her ear
The beauty of the world she holds dear
She is the Butterfly Child
Flying wild
Tonight, she'll be set free
Flying where she wants to be
Eternally
Across land and sea
She'll love you and she'll love me
If you treat her tenderly
Let her land
Then set her free
She'll come back eventually
The Wild One
Wings shining in the sun
Inspiring happiness
She's never done
Of her beautiful kind
She's the only one

Fly on Wild One
Be free
Kiss the clouds
Watch over me

UNCHAINED

Eleven steeples all in a row
But none of them are for you
All alone
A wanderer
Lone soul
No place to belong
Your temple is where you are
Your home is where you are
Your God is where you are
Your family is where you are
Your riches are where you are
A walking universe

THAT SHINE

Aquamarine eyes that cried crystal tears
Your gems have been buried
Their weight your shoulders carried
You gave the world your brilliant shine
If only, for a longer time
But gems like you are rare
And no one seemed to care
About consuming you
Possessing you
Stripping you bare
You had to close your eyes and sleep
Let Mother Nature hold you deep
Put your shine away for another day
Rest among the stars that equal your beauty
Your next pair of shoulders will carry such richness
Not all gems are rare, but their shine makes them brilliant

IV

PEACE, WISDOM AND TIME

<u>TIES</u>

Life on Jupiter doesn't seem so bad
When life on Earth can be so sad
Give endless love and you'll realize
That between us all are ties
I am you
And you are me
A universal family

MEDAL OF DISHONOR

The breeze on my skin causes irritation

You and I

We're nation against nation

Fighting and stabbing

Bleeding and wounded

Do we keep up this madness

Until our lives become muted?

Put down your arrow

And come to my side

The solution to our issues

Is just a matter of pride

TIME

Is time an enemy

Or is time a friend

Here I am

Here is the end

Did you think it would last?

Time the hourglass

The sands trickle down

Its silent sound

When fire calls urgently

You answer its embers

Time can leave you burned

Or cool as December

Decide where you stand

When time divides the line

Fall deep into its precipice

Or embrace the grand design

__KEY__

Another year walked

Upon the path of life

Beautiful memories

Even moments of strife

As you journey many steps more

Never forget, you're the key

To unlock any door!

<u>NOVA</u>

In between space and time

Your future and past align

Universal forces stretch and bind

The perimeter never ends

RIPPLE

I know that times are scary

But please friends, don't be wary

The thing to do is clear

Keep strong and persevere

Give support to those in need

And return every good deed

If we come together

Any storm we will weather

Respect and love

Will keep you rising above

Panic and hate

Burden with a heavy weight

The choice you see is very simple

Just one good act creates a ripple

SEARCHING

This is how I feel

A century turned steel

Hardened heart

Callous peel

Reality isn't all it seems

Want answers by any means

It is brightness that gives reveal

It is darkness that hides and steals

Help my heart so it may find its way

Give it direction

A place to stay

Don't take for granted new revelations

Keep them with you

Go forward without reservations

25

Twenty-five

What a time to be alive

But I wish I were five

A girl with no worries

Play all day in the yard

I wish being an adult

Wasn't so hard

Let the next twenty-five be better

Not gone in the blink of an eye

To the years of my youth

Like the waves you roll on by

<u>PEACE</u>

I strive to see a smiling face

Upon every person

Of every race

Worries gone

And problems few

You care for me

And I care for you

When the dust has settled

And injustice is gone

Let's come together

And sing the same song

A song about love

Let voices ring high

Peace can be made

When you and I try

GENERATION HARMONY

They call it Generation Harmony

Existing well beyond X, Y and Z

Alpa, Omega, Orion's belt

Many can't fathom

Its power can melt

Melt your mind, heart and soul

United entity

Not here to control

Generation Harmony is always nearby

Past, future and present

A circle, connected by tie

When it's time it will reach you

Nearing closer is the day

It's about rhythm of spirit

Your personal rhyme paves the way

Coming soon to a theatre nearest you

Is Generation Harmony

Here to make its grand debut

WISDOM

As I get closer to the light

My hair grows more white

My bones ache

More unclear is my sight

I've tried it all

Done everything I could

Time kissed me daily

And I understood

Like the seasons

My leaves change and fall astray

There is only one treasure

I've stored and protected from decay

It's the wisdom I've gained

With each passing day

There will come a time

When my treasure is stolen from it's safe

I better share this bounty now

Don't put my good knowledge to waste!

SECRET ANGEL

Looking down from above

A secret angel sends her love

Watching over those in need

A hungry mouth she helps to feed

With a gift she lends a helping hand

To all she can in every land

Secret Angel is blessing you

May times of solace be many

And times of worry be few

MY DEAREST READERS

Goodbye for now

We've reached the end of the book

I take my last bow

Waving to your reading nook

Thank you for spending time with me

I hope you've had a blast

I hope tonight's performance

Will not become our last

Journey away with me

When we do meet up again

In another book or so

Adieu, I'm off to get my pen

NOW THAT YOU'RE FEELING INSPIRED, THESE LAST PAGES ARE FOR YOU!

Write Out Any Creative Ideas Or Thoughts That Come Into Your Mind! Have Fun!

DO YOU HAVE A FAVORITE PLACE TO GO TO RELAX?

THIS PAINTING WAS INSPIRED BY ALL OF THE BEAUTIFUL SEASHELLS ON THE BEACH. SOME PEOPLE LOVE TO COLLECT SEASHELLS. WHAT DO YOU COLLECT?

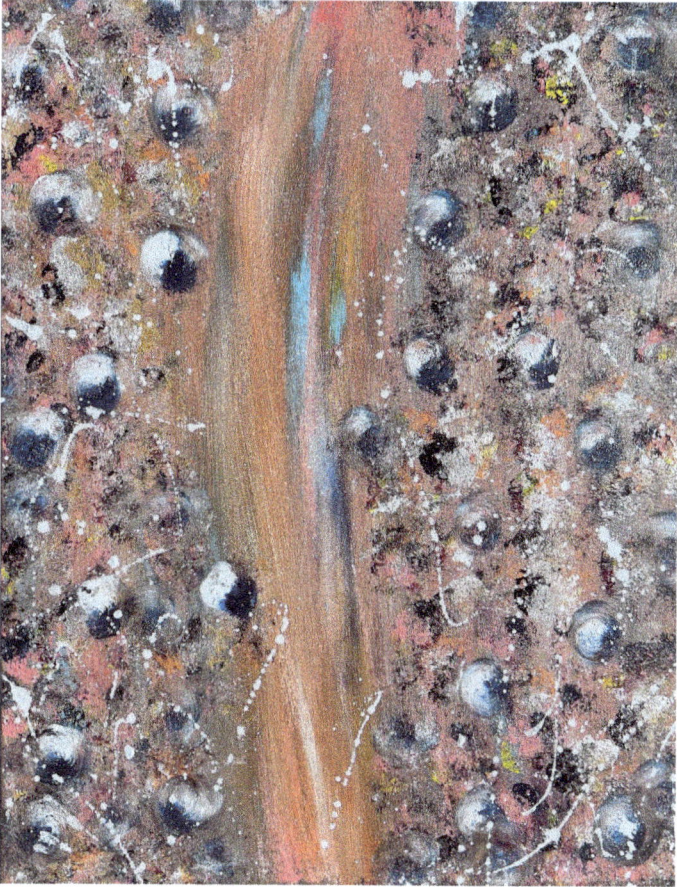

I BELIEVE THAT THE EARTH NEEDS DREAMERS TO ADD COLOR
TO THE WORLD AROUND US. WHAT ARE YOUR DREAMS?

DOGS ARE VERY SPECIAL TO ME AND HAVE BEEN SUCH
WONDERFUL COMPANIONS THROUGHOUT MY LIFE. DO YOU
HAVE ANY ANIMALS? WHO IS YOUR FAVORITE COMPANION?

DO YOU EVER WONDER WHAT IT WOULD BE LIKE TO VISIT SPACE? WHAT WOULD YOU LIKE TO SEE?

SOMETIMES WE GIVE OUR HEART AWAY TO ANOTHER AND WE NEVER KNOW WHAT THE OUTCOME WILL BE. IF THE OUTCOME IS HEARTBREAK, IT DOESN'T MEAN WE SHOULD STOP LOVING. LOVE IS THE GREATEST GIFT WE CAN SHARE! WHEN YOU THINK ABOUT LOVE, WHAT OR WHO COMES TO MIND?

I SOMETIMES LOOK UP AT THE MOON AND REFLECT UPON MY DAY. HOW WAS YOUR DAY TODAY?

I LOVE ART BECAUSE I CAN CREATE OTHER WORLDS WITH JUST MY PAINTBRUSH. IF YOU COULD CREATE YOUR OWN WORLD, WHAT WOULD IT LOOK LIKE?

DO YOU EVER WISH YOU COULD FLY? WHERE WOULD YOU TRAVEL TO?

I LOVE FLOWERS! THEY INSPIRE A LOT OF MY WRITING. DO YOU HAVE A FAVORITE FLOWER? WHAT DO YOU LOOK AT TO FEEL HAPPY?

SOMETIMES I REFLECT ON THE PATHS I'VE TAKEN TO BRING ME TO THE PRESENT MOMENT. DO YOU THINK YOU WOULD HAVE TAKEN ANY DIFFENT PATHS? WHAT PATHS DO YOU SEE FOR YOURSELF IN THE FUTURE?

DO YOU ENJOY THE ARTS? WHAT INSPIRES YOU? WHAT ARE
YOUR HOBBIES/ INTERESTS?

HOW DOES NATURE MAKE YOU FEEL?

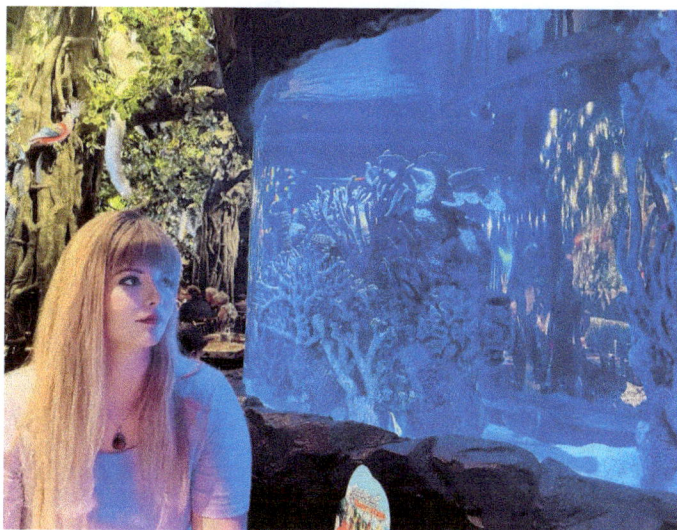

HAVING OUR OWN UNIQUE PERSONALITY MAKES US AN INDIVIDUAL. ONE ASPECT OF BEING A HUMAN IS HAVING EMOTIONS. MUSIC HAS THE ABILITY TO IMPROVE MY MOOD INSTANTLY. WHAT IS SOMETHING YOU USE TO HEAL YOUR EMOTIONS ON A TOUGH DAY?

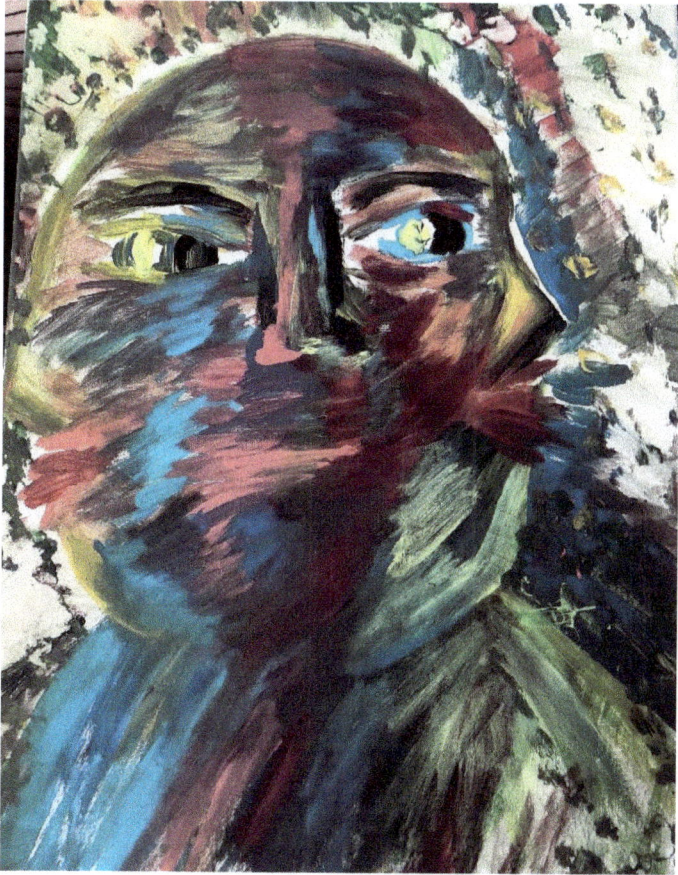

THIS PAINTING WAS INSPIRED BY AN OUTFIT PATTERN I SAW THAT REALLY STRUCK ME. WHAT IS YOUR FASHION STYLE?

www.ingramcontent.com/pod-product-compliance
Lightning Source LLC
Chambersburg PA
CBHW060351110426
42736CB00049B/2416